Dedication

"I would like to dedicate this program to all those who ever struggled with learning a foreign language"

Also by Yatir Nitzany

Conversational Spanish Quick and Easy
Conversational Portuguese Quick and Easy
Conversational Hebrew Quick and Easy

Conversational
French
Quick and Easy

THE MOST ADVANCED REVOLUTIONARY TECHNIQUE TO MASTER CONVERSATIONAL FRENCH

YATIR NITZANY

Copyright © 2012
Yatir Nitzany
All rights reserved.
ISBN-10: 1499102046
EAN-13: 9781499102048

Printed in the United States of America

FORWARD

ABOUT MYSELF

For many years I struggled to learn Spanish, and still knew no more than about 20 words and consequently was extremely frustrated. One day I stumbled upon this method as I was playing around with word combinations. Suddenly I came to the realization that every language has a certain core group of words that are most commonly used in a language, and simply by learning them, one could gain ability to engage in fluent communication..

I discovered which those words were, narrowed them down to 350, and that once memorized, one could then connect and create one's own sentences. THE VARIATIONS WERE and ARE, INFINITE!!! By using this incredibly simple technique I could converse at a proficient level and speak Spanish. Within a week I astonished my Spanish speaking friends with my new found ability. The next semester I registered at my university for a Spanish Speaking Course and I applied the same principles I learned in that class (grammar, additional vocabulary, future and past tense, etc.) to those 350 words I already had memorized. Immediately I felt as if I had grown wings and learned how to fly. At the end of the semester we took a class trip to San José, Costa Rica. I was like a fish in water, while the rest of my classmates were floundering and still struggling to converse. Throughout the following months I again applied the same principle to other languages, French, Portuguese, Italian, and Arabic all of which I now speak proficiently thanks to this very simple technique.

This method is by far the fastest way to master fluent conversation. There is no other technique that compares to my concept. It is effective, it worked for me and it will work for you. Be consistent with my program and you too will succeed the way I and many, many others have.

Contents

Introduction to the Program. 8

Introduction to the French Language 11

Memorization Made Easy 13

Note to the Reader 15

The Program 16

Building Bridges 38

Basic Grammatical Requirements of the
   French Language. 42

Other Useful Tools for the French Language 47

Now you are on your own 51

Conclusion 53

INTRODUCTION TO THE PROGRAM

People often dream about learning a foreign language, but never do. Whatever the reason is, it's time to set it aside and with my new method, you will have enough time and you will not fail. You will actually learn how to speak the fundamentals of the language, and speak the language fluently in as little as a few days. Of course you won't speak perfect French at first, but you will certainly gain significant proficiency. For example, if you travel to France or a French Speaking Country, you will almost effortlessly be able engage in basic 'fluent' communication with the locals, and you will no longer be intimidated with culture shock. It's time to relax. Learning a language is a valuable skill and a form of communication that connects people of multiple cultures around the world.

How does my method work? Well, I have taken twenty-seven of the most used languages and distilled out of them the 350 most commonly used words in any language. This whole process took three years of observation and research, and during that time I have determined which words I felt were most important for this method of basic 'fluent' communication. In that time, I chose these words in such a way that they are structurally interrelated, and when combined, they form sentences. Thus once you succeed in memorizing them, then you will be able to combine these words and form your own sentences. The words are spread over 20 pages. In fact, there are just nine basic words that will effectively build bridges, enabling you to speak in an

Introduction to the Program

understandable manner (please see *Building Bridges* on page #38). The words will also correspond easily in sentences, for example, enabling you to ask simple questions, etc. I have also created *Memorization Made Easy* techniques for this program in order to help with the memorization of the vocabulary (Page #13). Please also see page #47, in order to gain proficiency in the *Reading and Pronunciation of the French Language* , prior to starting this program.

    My book is intended mainly for basic 'present tense' vocal communication, meaning anyone can easily use it to 'get by' linguistically while visiting a foreign country, without learning the entire language. You will be 100 percent understandable to native speakers, which is your aim. One disclaimer: this is NOT a grammar book, though it does address minute and essential grammar rules (Please see Basic Grammatical Requirements of the French Language on page #42). Therefore, understanding complex sentences with obscure words in a language is outside the scope of this book.

    People who have tried this method have been successful, and by the time you finish this book, you will be 90 percent fluent and understandable in the French language. This is the best basis to learn, not only the French language but any language. THIS IS AN ENTIRELY REVOLUTIONARY NO-FAIL CONCEPT, and your ability to place all the pieces of the puzzle together, will come with GREAT ease, especially if you use this program prior to beginning a French class.

THE FRENCH LANGUAGE

The French language originated in France. It is a Romance language as are Spanish, Portuguese, Italian, and Romanian since they all descend from what originally was the spoken Latin language. Today, owing to France's colonial expansion between the 17th and 20th centuries there are now 29 countries where French is the official language. French is again rising in popularity. It has 16 million students and 220 million native speakers.

In the 16th century, King Francis I declared French as his nation's official language. Little did he know it was soon to become the 15th most common language in the world, and the official language of almost 30 countries. However, the language has declined in popularity since its peak in the 16th and 17th centuries. The French language was once used in diplomatic circles and was also a symbol of prestige, meaning only the nobility and higher classes of educated people spoke it. Russia's Catherine the Great and all her court communicated in French, as well as Prussia's Frederick II. Despite it's many dialects French is still spoken in all its former colonies.

Spoken in: France, Belgium, Switzerland, Luxembourg, Monaco, Benin, Burkina Faso, Burundi, Cameroon, Canada, Central African Republic, Chad, Comoros, Republic of the Congo, Democratic Republic of the Congo, Côte d'Ivoire, Djibouti, Equatorial Guinea, Gabon, Guiana, Guinea, Haiti, Madagascar, Mali, Niger, Rwanda, Senegal, Seychelles, Togo, and Vanuatu

MEMORIZATION MADE EASY

There is no doubt the 350 words in my program are the required essentials in order to engage in fluent basic conversation in any foreign language. However, some people may experience difficulty in the memorization, and for this reason I created "Memorization Made Easy," this memorization technique will make this program so simple and fun that it's unbelievable! I have spread the words over the following 20 pages. Each page contains a vocabulary table of 10-15 words. Below every vocabulary box, sentences are composed from the words, on the page, that you had just studied. This aids greatly in the memorization. Once you succeed in memorizing the first page, then proceed to the second, upon completion of the second page, go back to the first and review, then proceed to the third page, after memorizing the third go back to the first and second and repeat, and so on.... As you continue along, begin to combine words and create your own sentences in your head. Every time you proceed to the following page, you will notice words from the previous pages will be present in those simple sentences as well, as repetition is one of the most crucial aspects in learning any foreign language. Upon completion of the following twenty pages, CONGRATULATIONS!!! you have absorbed the required words and gained fluent proficiency, **and are now able to create your 'own'** sentences and be able to say anything you wish in the French language. THIS IS A CRASH COURSE IN CONVERSATIONAL FRENCH, AND IT WORKS!

NOTE TO THE READER

The purpose of this book is merely to enable you to communicate in French. In the program itself (pages 16-40) you may notice that the composition of some of those sentences might sound rather clumsy. Please disregard it, this is intentional. These sentences were formulated in a specific way to serve two purposes; to facilitate in the easy memorization of the vocabulary AND to teach you how to combine the words in order to form your own sentences for fluent communication, rather than making complete literal sense in the English language.

The sole purpose of this program is for conversational use ONLY, and is based on the method of the mirror translation technique. These sentences, as well as the translations are NOT incorrect, just a little clumsy. Latin languages, Semitic languages, Anglo-Germanic languages, as well as a few others are compatible with the mirror translation technique.

This method surpasses any other known language learning technique that is currently out there on the market. Just stick with the program and you will achieve wonders!!!!!

THE PROGRAM

Lets Begin! "Vocabulary"
(memorize the vocabulary)

I | I am	Je | Je suis
With you	Avec vous / Avec toi
With him / with her	Avec il / Avec elle
With us	Avec nous
For you	Pour vous / Pour toi
Without him	Sans lui
Without them	(Masc.) Sans eux / (fem)Sans Elles
Always	Toujours
Was	Etait
This	Ça, Ce, (Masc)Celui (Fem) Cela
Is	Est
Sometimes	Quelques fois / parfois
Maybe	Peut être
Are you	Êtes-vous / Es-tu
Better	Mieux / Meilleur
His / Hers	Que lui /qu'elle
He / She	Il / Elle
From	De

Sentences from the vocabulary (now you can speak the sentences and connect the words)

I am with you
Je suis avec toi

This is for you
C'est pour toi

I am from Canada
Je suis de Canada

Are you from Canada?
Êtes-vous de Canada?

Sometimes you are with us at the mall
Parfois tu es avec nous au mall

I am always with her
Je suis toujours avec elle

Are you without them today?
Êtes-vous sans eux aujourd'hui?

Sometimes I am with him
Quelques fois je suis avec lui

*Concerning the demonstrative *this* /Ça, Ce, Cela please see page #45
Mall is a universal known term in all languages, but the correct form of saying *mall* in French is *centre commercial*

Conversational French Quick and Easy

I was	J'étais
To be	Être
The	Le/ La/ Les / au
Same	Même
Good	Bon
Here	Ici
It's / it is	C'est / il est
And	Et
Between	Entre
Now	Maintenant
Later / After	Plus tard
If	Si
Yes	Oui
Then	Alors
Tomorrow	Demain
You	**(formal)** Vous/ **(informal)** tu
Also / too / as well	Aussi

Between now and later
Entre maintenant et plus tard
If it's later, then it is better tomorrow
Si c'est plus tard, alors il vaut mieux demain
This is good as well
C'est bon aussi
To be the same
Être le même
Yes, you are very good
Oui, vous êtes très bon
I was here with them
J'étais ici avec eux.
You and I
Vous et moi
The same day
Le même jour

*Concerning the formal and informal forms of *you*; *tu* and *vous*, please refer to page #43.
*The masculine form of the article *the* is *le*, the feminine form is *la*, and plural form is *les*. *Au* is *to the*. Please read #42 to learn more.

The Program

Me	Moi
Ok	Ok
Even if	Même si
Afterwards	Ensuite
Worse	Pire
Where	Où
Everything	Tout / tous
Somewhere	Quelque part
What	Quoi?
Almost	Presque
There	Là / là-bas

Afterwards is worse
Ensuite est pire
Even if I go now
Même si j'y vais maintenant?
Where is everything?
Où est tout?
Maybe somewhere
Peut être quelque part
What? I am almost there
Quoi? Je suis presque là
Where are you?
Vous êtes où?

Conversational French Quick and Easy

House	Maison
In	Dans / en
Car	Voiture
Already	Déja
Good morning	Bonjour
How are you?	Comment ça va?
Where are you from?	D'où vous venez?
Today	Aujourd'ui
Hello	Bonjour
What is your name?	Comment tu t'appelles?
How old are you?	Quel est votre âge?
Son	Fils
Daughter	Fille
At	À / à
Very	Très
Hard	Dur
Still	Encore

She is without a car, so maybe she is still at the house?
Elle n'a pas de voiture, alors peut-être qu'elle est encore à la maison

I am in the car already with your son and daughter
Je suis déjà dans la voiture avec ton fils et fille

Good morning, how are you today?
Bonjour, comment ça va aujourd'ui?

Hello, what is your name?
Bonjour, comment tu t'appelles?

How old are you?
Quel est votre age?

This is very hard, but it's not impossible
C'est très dur, mais ce n'est pas impossible

Where are you from?
D'où venez vous?

Thank you	Merci
For	Pour
Anything	Quelque chose
This is	C'est
Time	Temps
But	Mais
No / Not	Non
I am not	Je ne suis pas
Away	Loin
That	Ça (**M**) Ce, (**F**) Cela
Similar	Similaire
Other / Another	Autre / une autre
Side	Côté
Until	Jusque / jusqu'à
Yesterday	Hier
Without us	Sans nous
Since	Depuis
Day	Jour
Before	Avant

Thanks for anything
Merci pour quelque chose
It's almost time
C'est presque temps
I am not here, I am away
Je ne suis pas ici, je suis loin
That is a similar house
C'est une maison similaire
I am from the other side
Je suis de l'autre côté
But I was here until late yesterday
Mais j'étais ici jusque tard hier
Since the other day
Depuis l'autre jour

*Concerning the demonstrative *that* /*Ça, Ce, Cela* please see page #45

Conversational French Quick and Easy

I say / I am saying	Je dis que / Je suis en train de dire
What time is it?	Quelle heure est-il?
I want	Je veux
Without you	Sans toi
Everywhere /wherever	Partout / Partout où
I go / I am going	Je vais/ Je suis en train d'aller
With	Avec
My	**(Sing M/F)** Mon/Ma **(Plu)** Mes
Cousin	Cousin
I need	J'ai besoin
Right now	Maintenant
Night	Nuit
To see	Voir
Light	Lumière
Outside	Dehors
That is	C'est
Any	**(Sing)** Quelque **(Plu)** Quelques
I see / I am seeing	Je vois

I am saying no / I say no
Je suis en train de dire non / Je dis non
I want to see this during the day
Je veux voir cela pendant la journée
I see this everywhere
Je vois ça partout
I am happy without any of my cousins here
Je suis très content sans aucun de mes cousins ici
I need to be there at night
J'ai besoin d`être là la nuit
I see light outside
Je vois de la lumière dehors
What time is it right now?
Quelle heure est-il maintenant?

Place	Lieu
Easy	Facile
To find	Trouver
To look for / to search	Chercher
Near / Close	Près de
To wait	Attendre
To sell	Vendre
To use	Utiliser
To know	Savoir
To decide	Décider
Between	Entre
Two	Deux
To	À /à

This place is easy to find
Ce lieu est facile à trouver
I need to look for you next to the car
J'ai besoin de vous chercher près de la voiture
I am saying to wait until tomorrow
Je dis d'attendre jusqu'à demain
It's easy to sell this table
C'est facile de vendre ce tableau
I want to use this
Je veux utiliser ça
I need to know where is the house
J'ai besoin de savoir où est la maison
I need to decide between both places
J'ai besoin de décider entre les deux endroits
I need to know that everything is ok
J'ai besoin de savoir que tout est ok

That/which can also be used as relative pronouns, the translation in French is *que*. I need to know **that** everything is ok, j'ai besoin de savoir **que** tout est ok.

Conversational French Quick and Easy

Because	Parce que
To buy	Acheter
Both	Les deux
Them | They	(M) Eux (F) Elles / (M) Ils (F) elles
Their	Leurs
Book	Livre
Mine	À moi
To understand	Comprendre
Problem / Problems	Problème
I do / I am doing	Je fais/ Je suis en train de faire
Of	De
To look	Regarder
Myself	Moi même
Enough	Assez
Food	Nourriture
Water	Eau
Hotel	Hotel

I like this hotel because I want to look at the beach
J'aime cet hôtel parce je veux regarder la plage
I want to buy a bottle of water
Je veux acheter une bouteille d'eau
I do it like this each day
Je fais comme ça tous les jours
Both of them have enough food
Tous les deux ont suffisament de nourriture
That is the book, and that book is mine
C'est le livre, et ce livre est le mien
I need to understand the problem
J'ai besoin de comprendre le problème
From the hotel I have a view of the city
Depuis l'hôtel j'ai une vue de la ville
I can work today
Je peux travailler aujourd'hui
I do my homework
Je fais mes devoirs

*For the conjugation of *they have, ont* please refer to page #39 & 40

The Program

I like	J'aime
There is / There are	Il y a
Family / Parents	Famille/ Parents
Why	Porquoi
To say	Dire
Something	Quelque chose
To go	Aller
Ready	Prêt
Soon	Bientôt
To work	Travailler
Who	Qui
To know	Savoir

I like to be at my house with my parents
J'aime être à la maison avec mes parents
I want to know why I need to say something important
Je veux savoir pourquoi j'ai besoin de dire quelque chose d'important
I am there with him
Je suis là-bas avec lui
I am busy, but I need to be ready soon
Je suis occupé, mais j'ai besoin d'être prêt bientôt
I like to go to work
J'aime aller au travailler
Who is there?
Qui est là-bas?
I want to know if they are here, because I want to go outside
Je veux savoir s'ils sont ici, parce je veux sortir
There are seven dolls
Il y a sept poupées

*The literal meaning of *sortir* is *to go out*

Conversational French Quick and Easy

How much	Combien
To bring	Apporter
With me	Avec moi
Instead	À la place de
Only	Seulement
When	Quand
I can / Can I	Je peux
Or	Ou
Were	Étaient
Without me	Sans moi
Fast	Vite
Slow	Lentement
Cold	Froid
Inside	Dedans
To eat	Manger
Hot	Chaud
To Drive	Conduire

How much money do I need to bring with me?
Combien d'argent ai-je besoin d'apporter avec moi?
Instead of this cake, I like that cake
À la place de ce gâteau, j'aime l'autre gâteau
Only when you can
Seulement quand tu peux
They were without me yesterday
Ils étaient sans moi hier
I need to drive the car very fast or very slowly
J'ai besoin de conduire la voiture très vite ou très lentement
It is cold inside the library
Il fait froid à l'intérieur de la bibliothèque
Yes, I like to eat this hot for my lunch
Oui, j'aime manger ça chaud pour mon déjeuner

**Instead, à la place de* literally translates to *in place of*

To answer	Répondre
To fly	Voler
Today	Aujourd'ui
To travel	Voyager
To learn	Aprendre
How	Comment
To swim	Nager
To practice	Practiquer
To play	Jouer
To leave	Laisser
Many /much /a lot	Beaucoup
I go to	Je vais à
First	Premier
Time / Times	Fois

I need to answer many questions
J'ai besoin de répondre à beaucoup de questions
The bird must fly
L'oiseau doit voler
I need to learn to swim at the pool
J'ai besoin d'apprendre à nager à la piscine
I want to learn everything about how to play better tennis
Je veux tout savoir sur comment mieux jouer au tennis
I want to leave this here for you when I go to travel the world
Je veux laisser ça ici pour toi quand je vais voyager autour du monde
Since the first time
Depuis la première fois
The children are yours
Les enfants sont à vôtre

"In French the verb *to leave* has two meanings: *Laisser* and *Partir*
To leave (something), *laisser*. *To leave* (a place/ to go), *partir*.

Conversational French Quick and Easy

Nobody / Anyone	Personne
Against	Contre
Us	Nous
To visit	Rendre visite à
Mom / Mother	Maman/ Mère
To give	Donner
Which	Lequel
To meet	Rencontrer
Someone	Quelqu'un
Just	À peine
To walk	Marcher
Around	Autour
Towards	Vers
Than	Que
Nothing / Anything	Rien

Something is better than nothing
Quelque chose est mieux que rien
I am against him
Je suis contre lui
We go to visit my family each week
Nous allons rendre visite à ma famille chaque semaine
I need to give you something
J'ai besoin de te donner quelque chose
Do you want to meet someone?
Voulez-vous rencontrer quelqu'un?
I am here on Wednesdays as well
Je suis ici les mercredis aussi
You do this everyday?
Vous faites cela tous les jours?
You need to walk around, but not towards the house
Vous besoin de marcher autour mais non vers la maison

*In French *you want* is *vous voulez*, but ***do** you want* is *voulez-vouz*. Please refer to pages #39 and #40 to learn more

*In French, *which*, the masculine form is *Lequel / Laquelle* is the fem form/ *Lesquels* (Mpl) *Lesquelles* (Fpl)

The Program

I have	J'ai
Don't	Ne (...) pas
Friend	Ami (M) / Amie (F) / Amis (Mpl) / Amies (Fpl)
To borrow	Emprunter
To look like	Avoir l'air de / ressembler à
Grandfather	Grand père
To want	Vouloir
To stay	Rester
To continue	Continuer
Way	Chemin
That's why	C'est pourquoi
To show	Montrer
To prepare	Préparer
I am not going	Je ne vais pas

Do you want to look like Arnold
Voulez-vous ressembler à Arnold?
I want to borrow this book for my grandfather
Je veux emprunter ce livre pour mon grand père
I want to drive and to continue on this way to my house
Je veux conduire et continuer sur ce chemin jusqu'à chez moi
I have a friend, that's why I want to stay in Paris
J'ai un amie, c'est pour cela que je veux rester à Paris
I am not going to see anyone here
Je ne vais pas voir personne ici
I need to show you how to prepare breakfast
J'ai besoin de te montrer comment préparer le petit déjeuner
Why don't you have the book?
Pourquoi n'avez vous pas le livre?
That is incorrect, I don't need the car today
C'est incorrect, je n'ai pas besoin de la voiture aujourd'hui

*To make a verb negative add *ne* before the verb and *pas* after. Please see page #45 to learn more.

To remember	Se rappeler de
Your	(Sing)(M)Ton /(F)Ta (Plur)Tes
Number	Numéro
Hour	L'heure
Dark / darkness	Sombre / Oscurité
About	A / À propos / sur
Grandmother	Grand mère
Five	Cinq
Minute / Minutes	Minute / Minutes
More	Plus
To think	Penser
To do	Faire
To come	Venir
To hear	Écouter
Last	(M)Dernièr /(F)Dernière

You need to remember my number
Vous avez besoin de vous rappeler de mon numéro
This is the last hour of darkness
C'est la dernière heure d'obscurité
I want to come and to hear my grandmother speak French today
Je veux venir et écouter ma grand-mère parle français aujourd'hui
I need to think more about this, and what to do
J'ai besoin de penser plus à ça, et quoi faire
From here until there, it's only five minutes
D'ici jusque la, c'est seulement cinq minutes

To leave	Partir
Again	Encore
France	France
To take	Prendre
To try	Essayer
To rent	Louer
Without her	Sans elle
We are	Nous sommes
To turn off	Eteindre
To ask	Demander
To stop	Arrêter
Permission	Permission

He needs to leave and rent a house at the beach
Il a besoin de partir et louer une maison à la plage
I want to pass the test without her
Je veux passer le test sans elle
We are here a long time
Nous sommes ici depuis longtemps
I need to turn off the lights early tonight
J'ai besoin d'éteindre les lumières tôt ce soir
We want to stop here
Nous voulons nous arrêter ici
We came from Spain
Nous venons d'Espagne
The same building
Le même immeuble
I want to ask permission to leave
Je veux demander la permission de partir

*In French *night* is *nuit*, but *tonight* is *ce soir*

Conversational French Quick and Easy

To open	Ouvrir
To buy	Acheter
To pay	Payer
Last	Dernier
Without	Sans
Sister	Sœur
To hope	Espérer
To live	Vivre
Nice to meet you	Ravis de faire votre connaisance
Name	Prénom
Last name	Nom
To return	Retourner
Enough	Assez
Door	Porte

I need to open the door for my sister
J'ai besoin d'ouvrir la porte pour ma sœur
I need to buy something
J'ai besoin d'acheter quelque chose
I want to meet your sisters
Je veux rencontrer tes sœurs
Nice to meet you, what is your name and your last name?
Ravis de faire votre connaissance, quel est votre prénom et votre nom?
To hope for the better in the future
Espèrer le mieux pour l'avenir
I want to return from the United States and to live without problems in France
Je veux retourner aux États-Unis et vivre sans problèmes en France
Why are you sad right now?
Pourquoi êtes-vous triste maintenant?

*The plural form of *your* is *tes*. The masculine singular of *your* is *ton*, the feminine form is *ta*. The formal is *votre*. Read page #43 to learn more.

The Program

To happen	Arriver
To order	Commander
To drink	Boire
Excuse me	Excusez-moi
Child	Enfant
Woman	Femme
To begin / To start	Commencer
To finish	Finir
To help	Aider
To smoke	Fumer
To love	Aimer
To talk / To Speak	Parler

This must happen today
Cela doit arriver aujourd'hui
Excuse me, my child is here as well
Excusez-moi, mon enfant est ici aussi
I love you
Je vous aime
I see you
Je vous vois
I need you
J'ai besoin de vous
I need to begin soon to be able to finish at 3 o'clock in the afternoon
J'ai besoin de commencer bientôt pour pouvoir finir à 3 heures de l'après-midi
I want to help
Je veux aider
I don't want to smoke again
Je ne veux pas fumer encore
I want to learn to speak French
Je veux apprendre à parler Français

*The verb *must* and the verb *to have to* is *devoir*. Conjugation form; je dois, tu dois, il/elle/cela doit, nous devons, ils/elles doivent

Conversational French Quick and Easy

To read	Lire
To write	Écrire
To teach	Enseigner
To close	Fermer
To turn on	Allumer
To prefer / To choose	Préférer / Choisir
To put	Mettre
Less	Moins
Sun	Soleil
Month	Mois
I Talk	Je parle
Exact	Exacte

I need this book to learn how to read and write in French because I want to teach in France
J'ai besoin de ce livre pour apprendre á lire et écrire en Français parce que je veux enseigner en France
I want to close the door of the house and not to turn on the light
Je veux fermer la porte de la maison et ne pas allumer la lumière
I prefer to put the gift here
Je préfère mettre le cadeau ici
I want to pay less than you for the dinner
Je veux payer moins que vous pour le dîner
I speak with the boy and the girl in Spanish
Je parle avec le garçon et la fille en espagnol
There is sun outside today
Il y a du soleil dehors aujourd'hui
Is it possible to know the exact date?
Est-il possible de savoir la date exacte?

*In the English language, adjectives preceed the noun; for example *exact date*, but in French it's usually the opposite, *la date exacte*.

To exchange	Échanger
To call	Appeler
Brother	Frère
Dad	Papa
To sit	Asseoir
Together	Ensemble
To change	Changer
Of course	Bien sûr
Welcome	Bienvenue
During	Pendant
Years	Ans
Sky	Ciel
Up	Là-haut
Down	En bas
Sorry	Désolé (M) / Désolée (F)
To follow	Suivre
Her	Elle
Big	Grand
New	Nouveau
Never	Jamais

I never want to exchange this money at the bank
Je ne veux jamais échanger cet argent à la banque
I want to call my brother and my dad today
Je veux appeler mon frère et mon papa aujourd'hui
Of course I can come to the theater, and I want to sit together with you and with your sister
Bien sûr je peux venir au théâtre, et je veux m'asseoir ensemble avec vous et ta sœur
I need to go down to see your new house
J'ai besoin d'aller en bas pour voir ta nouvelle maison
I can see the sky from the window
Je peux voir le ciel depuis la fenêtre
I am sorry, but he wants to follow her to the store
Je suis désolé, il veut la suivre au magasin

To allow	Permettre
To believe	Croire
Morning	Matin
Except	Sauf
To promise	Promettre
Good night	Bonsoir/ Bonne soiree
To recognize	Reconnaître
People	Gens
To move	Déplacer / Déménager
Far	Loin
Different	Différent
Man	Homme
To enter	Entrer
To receive	Recevoir
Throughout	Tout au long de
Good afternoon	Bon apres midi
Through	À travers
Him / Her	(M)Le /Lui	(F)La /Elle

I need to allow him to go with us, he is a different man now
J'ai besoin de le laisser partir avec nous, il est un homme différent maintenant

I believe everything except for this
Je crois tout sauf cela

I must promise to say good night to my parents each night
Je dois promettre de dire bonne nuit à mes parents chaque nuit

They need to recognize the people from France very quickly
Ils ont besoin de reconnaître les gens de France très rapidement

I need to move your cat to another chair
J'ai besoin de déplacer ton chat à une autre chaise

They want to enter the competition and receive a free book
Ils veulent entrer dans la compétition et recevoir un livre gratuit

I see the sun throughout the morning from the kitchen
Je vois le soleil tout au long du matin depuis la cuisine

I go into the house but not through the yard
Je vais dans la maison mais pas par le jardin

The Program

To wish	Souhaiter
Bad	Mauvais
To Get	Obtenir
To forget	Oublier
Everybody / Everyone	Tout le monde
Although	Bien que
To feel	Sentir
Great	Grand
Next	Prochain
To like	Aimer
In front	Devant
Person	Personne
Behind	Derrière
Well	Bien
Goodbye	Au revoir
Restaurant	Restaurant
Bathroom	Les toilettes

I don't want to wish you anything bad
Je ne veux rien te souhaiter de mal
I must forget everybody from my past to feel well
Je dois oublier tout le monde de mon passé pour me sentir bien
I am next to the person behind you
Je suis à côté de la personne derrière toi
There is a great person in front of me
Il y a une grande personne devant moi
I say goodbye to my friends
Je dis au revoir à mes amis
In which part of the restaurant is the bathroom?
Dans quelle partie du restaurant sont les toilettes?
She has to get a car before the next year
Elle besoin d'acheter une voiture avant l'année prochaîne
I want to like the house, but it is very small
Je veux aimer la maison, mais elle est très petite

*Tout le monde literally translates into; *the entire world*, but the actual meaning is; *everyone* or *everybody*

Conversational French Quick and Easy

To remove	Enlever
Please	S'il vous plaît
Beautiful	Belle / jolie
To lift	Lever
Include / Including	Inclure
Belong	Appartenir
To hold	Tenir
To check	Vérifier
Small	Petit
Real	Vrai / Réel
Week	Semaine
Size	Taille
Even though	Quand même
Doesn't	Pas
So	Alors
Price	Prix

She wants to remove this door please
Elle veut enlever cette porte, s'il vous plaît
This doesn't belong here, I need to check again
Ça n'apartient pas ici, j'ai besoin de vérifier encore
This week the weather was very beautiful
Cette semaine le temps était très beau
I need to know which is the real diamond
J'ai besoin de savoir lequel est le vrai diamant
We need to check the size of the house
Nous avons besoin de vérifier la taille de la maison
I want to lift this, so you need to hold it high
Je veux lever ça, alors tu as besoin de le tenir haut
I can pay this although that the price is expensive
Je peux payer ça même que le prix est élevé
Including everything is this price correct?
Tout inclut c'est le prix correct?

BUILDING BRIDGES

In building bridges, we take these nine conjugated verbs, which have been selected after studies I have conducted for several months in order to determine which verbs are most commonly conjugated into first person, and which are then automatically followed by an infinitive verb. For example once you know how to say, *I Need, I Want, I Go, I Like,* it will enable you to say almost anything you want more proper and understandable.

I want	Je veux
I need	Je besoin
I can	Je peux
I like	J'aime
I go	Je vais
I have / I must	J'ai

*Avoir means *to have*, for example: *j'ai un appartement, I have an apartment*
Dois means *to have to* or *must*, for example: *je dois vois, I must see*

I want to go to my house
Je veux aller à ma maison
I can go with you to the bus station
Je peux aller avec vous à la station de bus
I need to walk to the muesum
J'ai besoin de marcher au musée
I like to take the train
J'aime prendre le train
I am going to teach a class
Je vais enseigner la classe
I have to speak to my teacher
Je dois parler à mon professeur

Please master pages #16-#38, prior to attempting the following two pages!!

You want / do you want	Tu veux / veux – tu
He wants / does he want	Il veut/ Veut-il?
She wants / does she want	Elle veut/ Veut - elle?
We want / do we want	Nous voulons/Voulons – nous?
They want / do they want	Ils / Elles Voulent / Voulent – elles/ ils?
You (plural/ formal sing)	Vous voulez /Voulez - vous?

You need / do you need	Tu as besoin / As – tu besoin?
He needs / does he need	Il a besoin / a –t- il besoin?
She needs / does she need	Elle a besoin / a – t- elle besoin?
We want / do we want	Nous avons besoin / avons – nous besoin?
They need / do they need	Ils/ Elles ont besoin/ ont – ils/ elles besoin?
You (plural/ formal sing)	Vous avez besoin/ Avez – vous besoin?

*In French, the verb " to need" always comes with the verb " to have" (avoir). In order to make a sentence, the verb "to have" must be conjugated.

You can / can you	Tu peux / Peux – tu?
He can / can he	Il peut / Peut – il?
She can / can she	Elle peut / Peut – elle
We can / can we	Nous pouvons / Pouvons – nous?
They can / can they	Ils / Elles peuvent / Peuvent – ils/elles?
You (plural/ formal sing)	Vous pouvez / Pouvez – vous?

You like / do you like	Tu aimes / Aimes – tu?
He likes / does he like	Il aime / Aime t –il?
She like / does she like	Elle aime / Aime t – elle?
We like / do we like	Nous aimons / Aimons – nous?
They like / do they like	Ils/ elles aiment / Aiment – ils/ elles
You (plural/ formal sing)	Vous aimez / Aimez – vous?

You go / do you go	Tu vas / vas – tu?
He goes / does he go	Il va / Va t – il?
She goes / does she go	Elle va / Va t –elle?
We go / do we go	Nous allons / Allons – nous?
They go / do they go	Ils/ elles vont / vont – ils/ elles?
You (plural/ formal sing)	Vous allez / Allez – vous?

You have / do you have	Tu as / As – tu?
He has / does he have	Il a / A t – il?
She has / does she have	Ell a / A t – elle
We have / do we have	Nous avons / Avons – nous?
They have / do they have	Ils/ elles ont / Ils / elles – ont?
You (plural/ formal sing)	Vous avez / Avez – vous

Building Bridges in French

Questions can be asked by inverting the conjugated verb and the subject pronoun, and then joining them with a hyphen. Example: *Do you want to read? / Veux - tu lire?*

Do you want to go?
Veux- tu aller?
Does he want to fly?
Veut – il prendre l'avion?
We want to swim
Nous voulons nager
Do they want to run?
Ils veulent courir
Do you need to clean?
Avez - vous besoin de nettoyer?
As - tu besoin de nettoyer?
She needs to sing a song
Elle besoin chanter une chanson
We need to travel
Nous avons besoin de voyager
They don't need to fight
Ils n'ont pas besoin de se battre
You (plural) need to see
Vous avez besoin de voir
Can you hear me?
Peux – tu m'écouter?
He can dance very well
Il peut dancer très bien
We can go out tonight
Nous pouvons sortir ce soir
They can break the wood
Ils peuvent casser du bois
Do you like to eat here?
Aimez – vous manger ici
Aime – tu manger ici

He likes to spend time here
Il aime passer du temps ici
We like to fix the house
Nous aimons réparer la maison
They like to cook
Ils aiment cuisiner
You (plural) like my house
Vous aimez ma maison
Do you go to school today?
Allez - vous à l'ecole aujourd'hui?
Vas – tu à l'ecole aujourd'hui
He goes fishing
Il va pêcher
We are going to relax
Nous allons nous détendre
They go to watch a film
Ils vont voir un film
Do you have money?
Avez - vous de l'argent?
As – tu de l'argent?
She must look outside
Elle doit regarder dehors
We have to sign our names
On doit signer avec notre noms
They have to send the letter
Ils / Elles doivent envoyer la lettre
You (plural) have to order
Vous devez commander

BASIC GRAMMATICAL REQUIREMENTS OF THE FRENCH LANGUAGE WHICH YOU WILL ENCOUNTER IN THIS PROGRAM

Feminine and Masculine & Plural and Singular

Every noun in the French language has a masculine or feminine gender. It's crucial to understand a noun's gender since both articles *the* and *a* are altered based on the gender of the noun they are pertaining to. *Le, the* is the masculine form and *la* is the feminine form of the article *the*. The plural form of the *le* and *la* is *les*.

The majority of words that conclude in a constant or *a* and *u* will end be masculine. For example *the sun, le soleil / the butterfly, le papillon.* French words, ending in *e, é, lle, on, eur, ble, cle, de, ge, me, ste, tre* will be considered feminine. For example; *The woman, la femme / the pool, la piscine / la cœur / the heart, the beach / la plage.*

Preceding a vowel, the *e* and the *a* from the article s *la* and *le* will be automatically eliminated. The article "*the*" will be *l'*; the(le) egg(oeuf), will be l'oeuf / the actor, l'acteur. Besides the vowels; *a,e,i,o* and *u*. The *h* , which is considered silent, isn't a vowel, but is occasionally treated according to the same grammar rules as if it was such. *The (le) man (homme),* will be *l'homme / the grass, l'herbe.*

In the French language the feminine form of *to the* and *at the* is *à la*, but the masculine form of *to the* is *au*. The same rule applies for *de*, the feminine form is *de la* but the masculine form is *du*.

Days of the week are not capitalized and are all in masculine form.

Basic Grammatical Requirements of the French Language

Pluralizing nouns

In French, in order to pluralize a noun an *s* must be added. There are a few exceptions though:
If the noun ends with an *eu, ou, eu, er* then add an *x* instead of an *s*. For example, *place, lieu*; (plural) *places* will be *lieux*.
If the noun ends with an *s* then nothing should be added. For example my *son, mon fils*; in plural *my sons* will be *mes fils*.
If there is an *al* or *il* at the end of the noun then replace it with *aux*. For example the newspaper, *il journal*; the newspapers will be *les journaux*.

Personal Pronouns

In regards to the pronoun *you*, there are two ways of saying it in French. **Vous** and **tu**;

Vous is the formal *you*. Use it when speaking to someone you just met, to authority, or to someone whom you are showing respect. *You* in plural is *vous* as well and you use it when, when speaking to a group of people or more than one person you use *vous*.

Tu is the informal *you*. Use it when speaking to a friend, acquaintance, relative, or close family member. Tu is a subject pronoun (second person of singular), refering to the individual who is doing the action.

Te is a direct and indirect object pronoun, the person who is actually affected by the action which is being carried out. But the *te* comes before the verb; *I need to show you, j'ai besoin de te montrer / I love you, je t'aime*.

Toi is a preposition pronoun, meaning it goes with a preposition; *with you, avec toi / for you, pour toi / after you, après toi*.

Votre is the formal *your*. **Vôtre** is the formal *yours*.
Vos is the plural formal form when refering to several objects; *your cars, vos voitures / your dogs, vos chiens*
Ton is the informal *your*, the informal feminine form is **ta**.
Tes is the infomal plural form.

43

Basic Grammatical Requirements of the French Language

Adjectives

In the English language adjectives proceed the noun, but in the French language, it's usually the opposite; *fast car* will be *voiture rapide, cold winter* will be *hiver froid.*
French adjectives are modified by the number and gender of the nouns which they are pertaining to. Every adjective can have four forms.
- To make a noun masculine you leave it the way it is
- To make it feminine just add an *e* at the end
- To make it plural masculine add an *s* at the end
- To make it plural feminine then simply add es at the end

For example *smart, intelligent* he is smart will be *il est intelligent, she is smart elle est intelligente,* plural masculine, *ils sont intelligents* / plural feminine, *ils sont intelligentes.* But if the adjective ends with an *s* or *x* then for masculine plural add nothing, but for feminine you must replace the *x* at the end with *se,* and for feminine plural you replace it with *ses; he is happy / il est heureux, she is happy / elle est heureuse, the boys are happy / les garçons sont heureux, the girls are happy / les filles sont heureuses*

Comparisons

In order to use comparisons add *plus* and *que.*
For example:
Better than / Plus mieux que
Darker than / Plus sombre que,
Stronger than / Plus forte que

Time

When referring to *time, il est une heure* means *it's one o'clock.* Any number greater than *one,* the *heure* becomes pluralized;
il est cinq heures / it's five o'clock, il est six heures / it's six o'clock

Basic Grammatical Requirements of the French Language

Verbs

French verbs are conjugated in a different form than English verbs.

To make a verb negative add *ne* before the verb and *pas* after.
For example:
I don't want. je ne veux pas
I don't see je ne vois pas
I can't je ne peux pas
I don't like je n'aime pas (since *aime*, *like* begins with a vowel, then the *e* in *ne* is eliminated and it connects to the verb with a hyphen)

*a contraction is used when the word which follows *ne* begins with a vowel)

Demonstratives

This, ceci and *that, cela* are the formal ways of reference to *this* and *that*. But instead use *ce* and *ça* which are the spoken form. Both **ce** (*cette* feminine tense of *ce* and *ces* is the plural of *ce* and *cette*) and **ça** could mean the same thing; *this, that, and it*.
  The difference between the two:
ce- usually goes with a noun, neutral, or the verb *être, to be*
Noun:
that place, ce lieu / that house, cette maison / these days, ces jours
Verb être, to be:
That is a boy, c'est un garçon
That is very easy, c'est très facile
It is not impossible, ce n'est pas impossible
  Since *is* is a form of the verb *to be*. *That is* or *this is* (both words connect) *ce +est =c'est*, "it's not" or "this/that is not" is "ce n'est".
  Neutral:
This idea, cette idée / that journey, ce voyage
Idea and *journey* are neuteral since they can be either male or female.

ça- usually goes with any other verb besides *être;*
I want this, je veux ça / I don't need this, je ne besoin pas ça.

* Both *ce* and *ça* can also be used before the verbs *pouvoir* and *devoir;*
This can be hard, ce peut être difficile/ this must happen, ce doit faire
This can be hard, ça peut être difficile/ this must happen, ça doit faire

45

OTHER USEFUL TOOLS FOR THE FRENCH LANGUAGE

Reading and Pronunciation
French pronunciation is rather different than English, because there are multiple ways in which letters can become silent. But if you follow these following steps it will help you in French pronuncation.
In general, most consonants in English and French sound the same.

ge and *gi* is pronounced as *je*
h is silent
qu is pronounced as *k*
ch is pronounced as *sh*
th is pronounced as *t*, rather than being pronounced as *th*
Ç and the *r* in the French language are letters which don't exist in English. The *ç* sounds like an *s*.
The French r on the other hand is pronounced at the back of your throat, unlike the *r* in English and Spanish.

Pronouncing Vowels in French
e - sounds like *a*
é - sounds like *ay* as in *day*
ê, è - sounds like *e* in *net*
i, y - sounds like *ee*
o, au, eau - sounds like the o in float
ou, u - sounds like oo in good

Diphthongs
ail - sounds like *i* in *night*
an, en, em - pronounced with a long nasal sound
oi - sounds like *wa*
oui - sounds like *wee*

Silent letters

The French language has silent letters, which can be divided into three categories:

- E muet / Elision
- H muet and aspiré
- Final consonants

In French, words that end with an *e*, the *e* is usually not pronounced, but the consonant that precedes it will be, for example; *belle* will be pronounced as *bell*, *porte* will be pronounced as *port*. The letter *h* is never pronounced and is silent.

The Elision Rule applies to words ending in *ce, je, me, te, se, de, ne, que*, in which the last letter is omitted, as long as the following word begins with a consonant, and both connect creating one syllable:
I love you, je t'aime
I have, j'ai,
I don't have, je n'ai pas

In the French language the final consonant is dropped. (For example: *Bijoux* will be pronounced as *bijou, tous* will be pronounced as *tou, veux* will be pronounced as *veu*), (except if there is a "*c*", "*f*" and "*l*" which are generally pronounced). In the event a noun or adjective is pluralized the *s* will be dropped as well. For example *cat, chat* will be pronounced as *cha* but in plural *chats* will be pronounced as *chat*. Another example: "*Dans*", meaning "*in*" will be pronounced as *dan* (the "*n*" should not be stressed too strongly). There are a few exceptions though; *avec, club, hiver, avril* and a few others as well.

The Liaison Rule is a situation in which a consonant at the end of a word, which would usually not be pronounced, is pronounced due to the fact that its followed by a word that begins with a vowel or silent *h*, in that situation the *s* or *x* will be pronounced as *z*. *The friends, les amis,* would be pronounced as *lez-amis, deux amis* will be pronounced as *deuz-amis*.

Conversational French Quick and Easy

Days of the Week

Sunday	Dimanche
Monday	Lundi
Tuesday	Mardi
Wednesday	Mercredi
Thursday	Jeudi
Friday	Vendredi
Saturday	Samedi

Seasons

Spring	Printemps
Summer	Été
Autumn	Automne
Winter	Hiver

Colors

Black	Noir
White	Blanc
Gray	Gris
Red	Rouge
Blue	Bleu
Yellow	Jaune
Green	Vert
Orange	Orange
Purple	Violet
Brown	Marron

Numbers

One	Un
Two	Deux
Three	Trois
Four	Quatre
Five	Cinq
Six	Six
Seven	Sept
Eight	Huit
Nine	Neuf
Ten	Dix

Cardinal Directions

North	Nord
South	Sud
East	Est
West	Ouest

49

CONGRATULATIONS, NOW YOU ARE ON YOUR OWN!

From here the only thing left is to make improvements. Once the memorization of these 350 words has been attained one way of progression is by attending a French language class. By doing so, it will assist you in putting the grammar in place since beginner language classes generally teach mostly grammar. However, with what you have already learned, it will all be MUCH easier.

CONCLUSION

CONGRATULATIONS, you have completed all the tools needed to master the French language and I hope that this has been a valuable learning experience. Now you have sufficient communication skills to be confident enough to enbark on a visit to a French speaking county, impress your friends, and boost your resume so GOOD LUCK.

This program is available in other languages as well and it is my fervent hope that my language learning programs will be used for the good and will enable people from all corners of the globe, from all cultures and religions to be able to communicate harmoniously.

Made in the USA
Lexington, KY
16 January 2015